What do I do With a
Negative Thought?

Written by: Fiona Maria Williams

Illustrated by: Tamara Hackett

REVIEWS

"What do I do with a Negative Thought" is a fresh and creative approach for children to develop understanding and take command of their thoughts and feelings. The positive message in this book is likely to reduce anxiety and build resilience in children of all ages. The adults in their lives will also benefit from the insightful tips for caregivers. I highly recommend this book as an effective tool in promoting a healthy self-concept in our youth and future leaders"
- Dr. Dana Marrocco, Licensed School Psychologist & Author of "The Top Ten Lies We Tell Ourselves"

"As someone who struggled with anxiety, fear and negative thinking as a child, I wish I had this book! Learning what to do with negative thoughts is an often overlooked life skill. Whether your child gets caught up in negative thoughts or you simply want to empower them with this important skill, *"What do I do With a Negative Thought"* will serve them greatly in their growth and development. Every child can benefit from reading this book!"
- Corinne Zupko, Ed.S., award-winning author of "From Anxiety To Love"

"What do I do with a Negative Thought?" is a gorgeous new children's book, peppered with adorable illustrations. It was created to teach kids they have a choice about how to deal with negative thoughts. If only this was around when I was young! I remember spending hours dreading school events or thinking scary thoughts. So giving a child the knowledge and power to deal with thoughts in a different way will be life changing.
The book is written for a parent or teacher to read alongside the child. I love this format as it creates dialogue at home, or school, around the idea that thoughts are just like clouds, which you can either grab onto or let them pass on by. This book teaches a fantastic skill that isn't taught in mainstream education and will contribute hugely towards forming a positive belief system. All children should be issued one on birth!
- Frances Verbeek, Founder of the Happi Empire

Published by: Call to Mind Books

Authored by: Fiona Maria Williams

Illustrated by: Tamara Hackett

For more by Fiona please visit: www.healthyhappyminds.ca

ISBN: 978-1-989394-01-4

Dedication:

To every child in the world.

This book is for YOU.

You will learn how to handle negative thoughts with ease.
Know that you deserve to be happy, creative
and to comfortably be your loving self.

To this day, when I face a challenge, my parents still remind me that
I can move onward and upward, and so can YOU!

Love and Healthy Thinking,
Fiona

Introduction for Parents, Caregivers and Teachers

This book was created to teach children how to manage the negative, fearful thoughts they will experience as they grow up. As you will see, the teachings in this book will help children understand that we all have negative thoughts and that it is possible to overcome them healthfully. They will learn that the best thing to do with negative thoughts is to let them go by in peace. This will help children avoid creating negative thinking habits which will only degrade their self-esteem and lead to an unhealthy perception of themselves, others and the world. Every moment is an opportunity for children to practice creating healthy thinking habits which promote love, peace and creativity.

These teachings will also support children in handling challenges. Being unnecessarily preoccupied with fear thoughts is what clouds us from seeing the lessons behind our challenges. Author and Teacher, Eckhart Tolle teaches that we all face our challenges, but it is our negative thinking which makes us think that challenges are really "problems." My intention is to encourage children to practice detaching from negative thinking so they will see the lessons in their challenges clearly without them turning them into unnecessary problems.

As an example, say a child is made fun of by another child. Initially, they may be offended and they will feel attacked and upset. If they get caught up in these negative feelings, they will continue to feel upset for a long period of time and may see the other child as an enemy. Yet, if they learn to feel their feelings safely and practice letting the insult and the negative thoughts about the incident pass by without further investment, they will be more relaxed and confident in themselves. As a result, they will learn to see the situation more clearly and may even begin to feel compassion for the other child. Maybe they could even become friends? The truth is, no one will ever see the opportunities for peace and happiness if they keep thinking negatively.

Overcoming fear positively is an essential skill for a healthy life! As children grow and develop into teenagers then adults, they will always have a choice to focus on negativity or learn from the lessons presented to them, create healthy thinking habits and develop coping mechanisms which help them through challenging times. With consistent practice, they can become confident, emotionally intelligent and compassionate.

In the children's portion of the book, you will find instructional guidelines (in a small rectangle on its own page) which follow four of the teachings of "What NOT to do with a Negative Thought." They are an elaboration of the teaching so you, the parent, caregiver or teacher, can help children understand the teaching fully.

Now...let's begin

What is a Negative Thought?

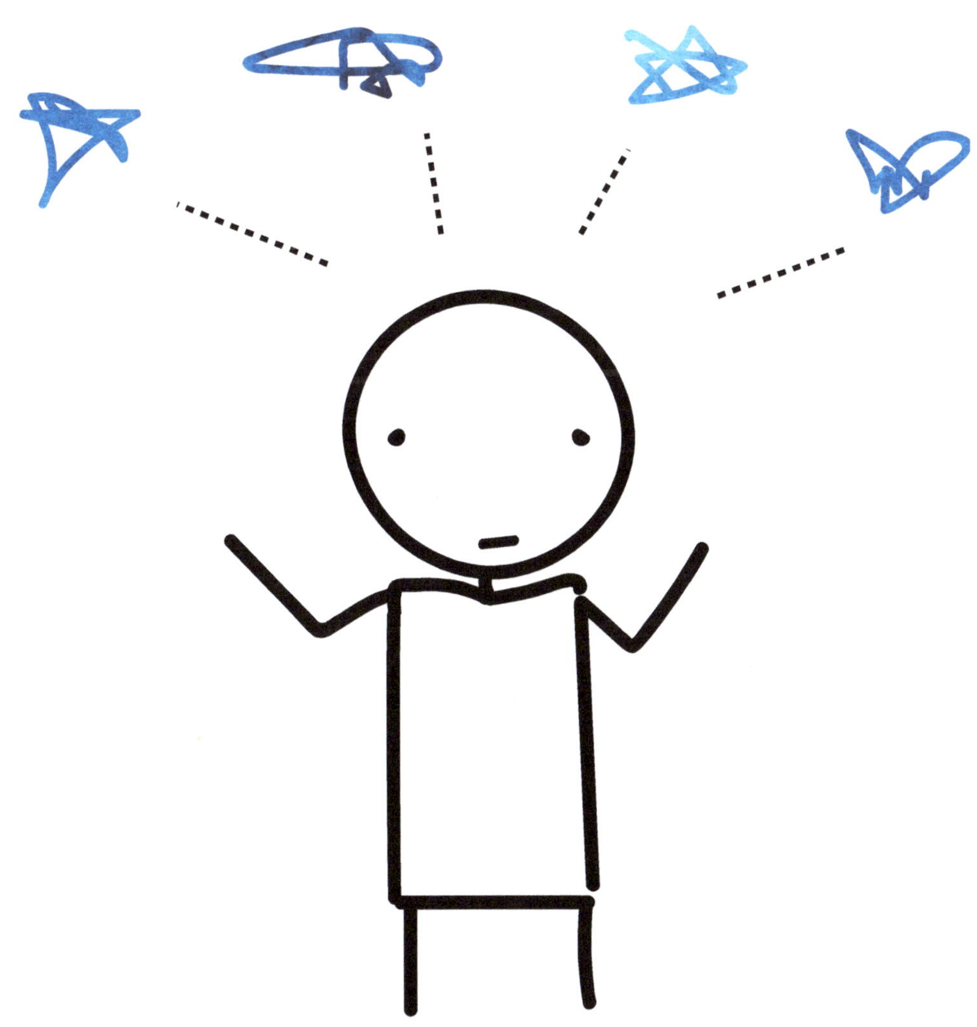

It's a thought that, when you think of it,

you become scared, sad or angry.

Negative thoughts can pop out and SURPRISE you!

Sometimes they are there when you wake up!

That hurt my feelings...

Today is going to be bad..

I'm no good...

I wish I didn't do that...

I can't do it...

No one will talk to me today...

yawn...

I remember..

And then they seem

to follow you throughout the day.

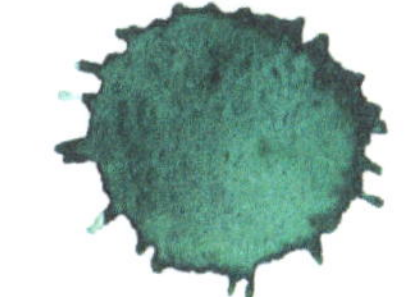

Everyone thinks negative thoughts.

But, here's a secret not everyone knows...

Just because you think a negative thought, does not mean that you have to keep thinking about it!

You see, your thoughts grow stronger the more you repeat them

So, the more you keep thinking about the scary, sad or angry thoughts, the

bigger and stronger they will become!

And the bigger and stronger they are, the more they will cloud over your happy and loving thoughts.

To help you think happier thoughts,

you have to practice not paying attention to negative thoughts!

So, here's what NOT to do with a negative thought!

You don't want to follow it to see where it might go!

Upon thinking a negative, fearful thought, a child can easily let their mind wander down an erroneous path. Children can follow negative thinking and as a result, get quite upset and anxious. Typically, negative thinking involves worrying about the future where children can ask themselves, "What if this happens?" Then, "Oh my goodness! What if that happens?" Following a negative thought can also present itself as a child rehashing distressing events about the past. Either way, negativity is being strengthened by the child following the initial fearful thought down an upsetting path.

You also don't want to defend yourself against the negative thought.

Some negative thoughts are so frightening that children will feel inclined to defend themselves against them. Being defensive is a way of acknowledging a negative, fear thought as real. Therefore, every time a child is defensive, the fear thought and their defenses will become stronger and they will not feel genuinely peaceful.

Be sure to NOT make friends with it!

In this instance, we want to help children to not identify with the negative thought. Judging themselves or others negatively, or seeing an insult as true are ways they "make friends" with a negative thought. Once they identify with a negative thought, it will be easier for the child to think of it and it will get stronger in their mind. This also includes any fear they are holding onto about a certain situation, person or place.

Yet, you also DON'T want to yell at it and make it your enemy.

It is common to think that telling a negative, fearful thought to "go away" or to get mad at it, is a good way to get rid of it. This is not the case. Acknowledging a negative thought in any manner makes the thought real in the mind and the thought is therefore strengthened.

Most importantly,

you don't need to believe in the negative thought!

Instead, you can choose to do this with a negative thought...

Let it float by you, just like a cloud in the sky.

Letting the negative thought go by you peacefully,

makes sure that you are not keeping it or repeating it,

and so you're not letting it get stronger.

Now, sometimes we will feel sad, scared or angry because we believed

in the negative thought...

Know that just because you may have these feelings, you still don't need to hold onto the negative thought which caused them. You always have a choice to let the negative thought go when you're ready to!

When you're UPSET,

here are some things you can do to feel better...

You can ask someone you trust for a hug.

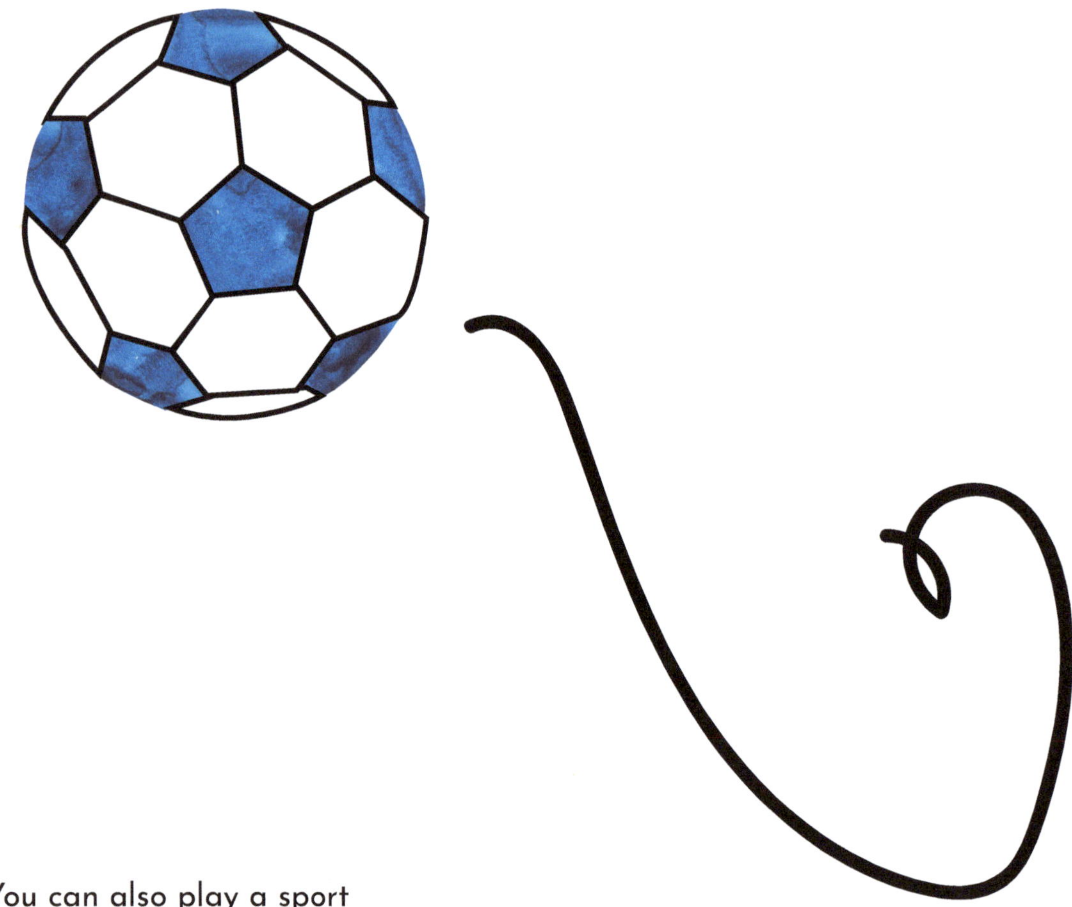

You can also play a sport

or do a favourite dance...

maybe even sing!

Or, if you want to do something quieter,

you can relax and take a few deep breaths

while thinking of something you love.

All of these things will help you

let go of a negative thought quicker.

Your loving, happy and creative thoughts are waiting for you!

I am good...

I can do it...

Today is exciting...

She was nice today...

I like myself...

I remember...

Happy things can happen today...

What Do I Do with a Negative Thought? ~ Parent's Guide

There is an underlying thought which permeates the mind and that is the thought of love. Within any thought of love resides the benign qualities of peace and joy. When we think consistently with love, we are compassionate, creative and confident. I believe it is beneficial to teach children how to overcome fear healthfully so they are better able to focus on their authentic selves.

As adults, we are aware of the powerful and sometimes paralyzing effects of fear. Children become aware of fear by observing others but also through their own imaginations where they may convince themselves that a ghost lives in their closet or that a boogeyman lies in wait under their bed. I understand that it seems harmless enough, even laughable, to think of a child worry about an encounter with a boogeyman. Surely these types of fears could be deemed as a "right-of-passage" to becoming a teenager.

Nonetheless, fear can be debilitating due to the minds immense ability to imagine, and for this reason, fear will wear many masks but will still have the same debilitating effects. To the mind, fear is fear and therefore, being afraid of another child at school is just as terrifying as worrying about a supposed boogeyman lurking in a darkened corner.

WHERE FEAR COMES FROM

Fear comes from what is commonly referred to as the "ego mind" or "wrong mind." This part of the mind is really just an untrained part of our minds. Being untrained, this small part of the mind behaves like anything which is undisciplined; it is chatty, erratic and thrives off of conflict. It is the antithesis of peace. Paying attention to this part of the mind leads to behaviour and actions which are unhealthy and reinforce fear. Take heart that it is possible to calm and eventually overcome this part of the mind. Doing so simply requires commitment and discipline.

The majority of our minds is actually quite peaceful, it just doesn't seem that way because the ego mind is so loud and intrusive. We pay attention to fear and think that it's all there is, only because it is so piercing. Also, our bodies respond to fear and this response gives us "evidence" that the fear thought must be real. Therefore, the experience of fear is quite powerful but the intensity diminishes as we practice dissociating from the fear.

HOW FEAR IS REINFORCED

All of our thinking patterns are habitual and fear thoughts are no different. The one thing which keeps fear alive in the mind is repetition. Through repetition, our thoughts turn into our beliefs. Repeating fear thoughts makes them more believable and leaves the mind susceptible to more fear-based thinking. Whatever we believe is what we have taken seriously, as belief is the breath of life for our thoughts. Thoughts can only affect us if we take them seriously.

How thoughts are unintentionally repeated is at the core of this book. Your child will learn all the ways in which fear thoughts can be repeated in their mind in the section titled What NOT to do with a negative thought.

They will be taught not to...
~ Don't follow it to see where it might go - When we are in fear mode, we will continue to think fearfully. It is good practice that when someone recognizes fear thoughts, that they stop, make an effort to calm down and correct the trajectory of their thinking. Essentially, when a child is afraid, we don't want them to continue thinking about anything other than calming down.

~ You don't want to defend yourself against it - Defense against a fear thought is easy to do as a conditioned response because it offers us a sense of protection. Yet this cozy feeling of protection is false and brief. Defense against the fear thought makes the fearful idea seem even more real in the mind and so it is best to take the time to move out of the fear safely as opposed to defending against it.

~ You also don't want to make friends with it - It is a common belief that people should make friends with their fears. I will cover this in a later section which teaches that there is no such thing as a "healthy fear." Essentially, if it disrupts your child's peace of mind, it's not serving them well.

~ You don't want to get mad at it and make it an enemy - Another common belief is to have a child tell a fear thought to "go away!" Encouraging a child to get angry with a fear thought and yell at it is not helpful in the long run because if they are responding to it then they have made the fear thought real. Also, responding with anger is a fear response so instead of taking steps to move out of the fear, your child is remaining fearful. Remember, this is about overcoming fear, not giving in to it in any form. We all know the old adage, what we resist, persists.

~ You don't want to believe in the negative thought - Lastly, you want to help your child relinquish their belief in thoughts which hurt them. This is not pulling the wool over their eyes as you can always educate them about being safe in the world, but it's about helping them relinquish their belief in fear itself.

HOW TO OVERCOME FEAR

The ego mind is very complex and so, in order to overcome fear, all that is required is some simplicity in the form of relaxation techniques. Practices like mindfulness and meditation are helpful and are even part of the recovery process for people who are facing anxiety, depression and even post-traumatic stress disorder as these practices help to calm and focus the mind so the thought processes are not erratic and negatively-focused. For children, we can encourage the use of these practices to help strengthen the calmer part of their mind and we can also guide them on how to overcome the trickier moments of heightened fear.

The essential key to overcoming fearful thoughts, is simply to not reinforce them. To practice steering clear of unintentionally reinforcing fear-based thoughts here are two fundamentals of the mind which would be helpful for you to know:

1. Our minds can only think one thought at a time
2. A thought can only be one of two things, loving or fearful

Considering that our minds can't think of fear and love at the same time, we need to choose between one or the other. Therefore, we can encourage children to focus upon something more benign like breathing deeply or noticing the colours which they see around them. Putting their energy into practicing this technique creates the habit of switching from fear to love and is more effective than analyzing what is making them feel scared. Analyzing a fear thought keeps the mind stuck in fear and our aim is to help children move out of the fear safely. As you encourage your child to focus on one positive thought at a time, their mind will calm as they will have stopped fueling the fear thought.

Specifically, your approach to helping your child overcome fear will occur in two stages:

1. Help them calm down
2. Support them in distracting themselves with a new positive-based task

Assisting your child with regulating their emotions is an essential first step! Nothing will be accomplished if they are amped up and so they do require that safe space to move through their feelings. Let them know that they are loved and fully capable of getting through the fearful moment and that you are there to help them. Next, implement some calming techniques. If you and your child already have some favourite calming techniques in your toolbelt, awesome! Use them as needed, remembering that repetition is key to success.

One of my favourite coping mechanisms for getting out of fear is deep breathing. As simplistic as it may seem, deepening your breath accomplishes both the calming aspect required to overcome fear and also, by focusing on your breath your mind is distracted from the fear. You can begin by having your child place their awareness on their breathing and then ask them to slow it way down. Specifically, they want to take nice deep breaths or what I like to call "big belly breathing." They can place their hand on their stomach and feel it expand as they take a deep breath in and then feel their stomach contract as the air comes out. Alternatively, they can lay down and watch their stomach expand and contract. Both of these approaches help to immerse children in the experience of relaxation. Another benefit is their body will also begin to relax and their whole being will begin to normalize.

Once the child is calm, you can begin to implement the second phase of overcoming fear, distracting them with something fun, light-hearted and/or creative. You can invite them to watch a funny show, do a favourite craft, read, or do something outside especially if it is sunny. The key in this second phase is to ensure that they are engaged in a positive activity, in this regard, competitive or violent video games is not the type of distraction that would be helpful. You want to find something which will cut through the lower energy of fear and help your child to lighten up. They can practice doing this with every type of fear thought they encounter and in time, they will have some amazing and healthy coping mechanisms as their go-to habit instead of giving in to the fear!

As we all know, some fear responses are going to be stronger than others, so some fears may require more hand holding and more time to overcome. Always know though, that helping them to calm down and reorient back to the positive mindset is far more helpful to the child than staying in the fear.

"BUT, WHAT ABOUT HEALTHY FEARS?"

Fear is a misuse of the mind, and this is the case for all of us. No exceptions. Hear me when I say there is no such thing as a "healthy fear" - that's an oxymoron as there is nothing healthy about fear. The alternative is having a healthy respect for things which we're uncertain of like wild animals, traffic, fire and such. It's always helpful to have an awareness of your surroundings, of how things work and how they can be used safely, but children do not need to learn about these things through fear. If we attempt to educate using fear all this does is strengthen fear in your child's mind and they will miss the "why" they should or shouldn't do something. Providing them with the essential information they need to understand the new learning will help them engrain the lesson in their mind. If fear is used to teach the lesson, they may get curious and try to figure out the "why" they shouldn't do something on their own while in an unsafe situation.

MOTIVATING YOUR CHILD

To develop your child's motivation to do this work, it is helpful to acknowledge where they have already overcome fear before. Perhaps they were able to speak in front of their classroom or go down to the basement alone. Whatever challenge you can think of that they've successfully accomplished can be used as evidence that they have overcome fear before and they can certainly do it again!

As you create the practice of overcoming fear with your child, you can help them create awareness around what their triggers are. This new awareness will help them not to feel blind-sided by fear as they begin to recognize what stresses them out and what fear feels like in their body. They can then learn not to react but to implement a calming coping mechanism instead. This places them in a power position where they are aware of things but not giving in to them.

It is also helpful to try your best to maintain an emotionally consistent environment. Of course, upsets are going to happen at home but when you set the intention of having a calm environment, children will know what to expect and come to view their home as a sanctuary, a safe place where they can relax, create, learn and be silly. Consistent calm behaviour from you will help them to develop trust and your peaceful demonstration will be of great service to them as they grow.